YouDeserve Publications

I0476367

MUTUAL
World

All about Mutual Funds Investing
Understanding Mutual Funds
Key tools to analyse Mutual Funds

SANDY WRIGHT

Preface

Savings form an important part of the economy of any nation. With savings invested in various options available to the people, the money acts as the driver for growth of the country. This financial scene too presents multiple avenues to the investors. Though certainly not the best or deepest of markets in the world, it has ignited the growth rate in mutual fund industry to provide reasonable options for an ordinary man to invest his savings.Investment goals vary from person to person. While somebody wants security, others might give more weight age to returns alone. Somebody else might want to plan for his child's education while somebody might be saving for the proverbial rainy day or even life after retirement. With objectives defying any range, it is obvious that the products required will vary as well. **Guide Me!!** We help Beginners as well as investors to learn and analyze mutual fund performance indicators

Table of Content

MUTUAL FUNDS: UNIVERSAL APPEAL

Savings form an important part of the economy of any nation. With savings invested in various options available to the people, the money acts as the driver for growth of the country. Indian financial scene too presents multiple avenues to the investors. Though certainly not the best or deepest of markets in the world, it has ignited the growth rate in mutual fund industry to provide reasonable options for an ordinary man to invest his savings.

Investment goals vary from person to person. While somebody wants security, others might give more weight age to returns alone. Somebody else might want to plan for his child's education while somebody might be saving for the proverbial rainy day or even life after retirement. With objectives defying any range, it is obvious that the products required will vary as well.

Though still at a nascent stage, Indian MF industry offers a plethora of schemes and serves broadly all type of investors. The range of products includes equity funds, debt, liquid, gilt and balanced funds. There are also funds meant exclusively for young and old, small and large investors. Moreover, the setup of a legal structure, which has enough teeth to safeguard investors' interest, ensures that the investors are not cheated out of their hard-earned money. All in all, benefits provided by them cut across the boundaries of investor category and thus create for them, a universal appeal.

Investors of all categories could choose to invest on their own in multiple options but opt for mutual funds for the sole reason that all benefits come in a package.

Let us see how.

An investor normally prioritizes his investment needs before undertaking an investment. So different goals will be allocated different proportions of the total disposable amount. Investments for specific goals normally find their way into the debt market as risk reduction is of prime importance. This is the area for the risk-averse investors and here, mutual funds are generally the best option. The reasons are not difficult to see.

One can avail of the benefits of better returns with added benefits of anytime liquidity by investing in open-ended debt funds at lower risk. Many people have burnt their fingers by investing in fixed deposits of companies who were assuring high returns but have gone bust in course of time leading to distraught investors as well as pending cases in the Company Law Board.

This risk of default by any company that one has chosen to invest in, can be minimized by investing in mutual funds as the fund managers analyze the companies' financials more minutely than an individual can do as they have the expertise to do so. They can manage the maturity of their portfolio by investing in instruments of varied maturity profiles. Since there is no penalty on pre-mature withdrawal, as in the cases of fixed deposits, debt funds provide enough liquidity. Moreover, mutual funds are better placed to absorb the fluctuations in the prices of the securities as a result of interest rate variation and one can benefits from any such price movement.

Apart from liquidity, these funds have also provided very good post-tax returns on year to year basis. Even historically, we find that some of the debt funds have generated superior returns at relatively low level of risks. On an average debt funds have posted returns over 10 percent over one-year horizon. The best performing funds have given returns of around 14 percent in the last one-year period. In nutshell we can say that these funds have delivered more than what one expects of debt avenues such as post office schemes or bank fixed deposits. Though they are charged with a dividend distribution tax on dividend payout at 10 percent (plus a surcharge of 10 percent), the net income received is still tax free in the hands of investor and is generally much more than all other avenues, on a post tax basis.

Moving up in the risk spectrum, we have people who would like to take some risk and invest in equity funds/capital market. However, since their appetite for risk is also limited, they would rather have some exposure to debt as well. For these investors, balanced funds provide an easy route of investment. Armed with the expertise of investment techniques, they can invest in equity as well as good quality debt thereby reducing risks and providing the investor with better returns than he could otherwise manage. Since they can reshuffle their portfolio as per market conditions, they are likely to generate moderate returns even in pessimistic market conditions.

Next come the risk takers. Risk takers by their very nature, would not be averse to investing in high-risk avenues. Capital markets find their fancy more often than not, because they have historically generated better returns than any other avenue, provided, the money was judiciously invested. Though the risk associated is generally on the higher side of the spectrum, the return-potential compensates for the risk attached.

Capital markets interest people, albeit not all for there are several problems associated. First issue is that of expertise. While investing directly into capital market one has to be analytical enough to judge the valuation of the stock and understand the complex undertones of the stock. One needs to judge the right valuation for exiting the stock too. It is very difficult for a small investor to keep track of the movements of the market. Entrusting the job to experts, who watch the trends of the market and analyze the valuations of the stocks will solve this problem for an investor. Mutual funds specialize in identification of stocks through dedicated experts in the field and this enables them to pick stocks at the right moment. Sector funds provide an edge and generate good returns if the particular sector is doing well.

Next problem is that of funds/money. A single person can't invest in multiple high-priced stocks for the sole reason that his pockets are not likely to be deep enough. This limits him from diversifying his portfolio as well as benefiting from multiple investments. Here again, investing through MF route enables an investor to invest in many good stocks and reap benefits even through a small investment. This not only diversifies the portfolio and helps in generating returns from a number of sectors but reduces the risk as well. Though identification of the right fund might not be an easy task, availability of good investment consultants and counselors will help investors take informed decision.

Risk Tolerance/Return Expected	Focus	Suitable Products	Benefits offered by MFs
Low	Debt	Bank/Company FD, Debt based Funds	Liquidity, Better Post-Tax returns
Medium	Partially Debt, Partially Equity	Balanced Funds, Some Diversified Equity Funds and some debt Funds, Mix of shares and Fixed Deposits	Liquidity, Better Post-Tax returns, Better Management, Diversification

		Capital Market, Equity Funds (Diversified as well as Sector)	Diversification, Expertise in stock picking, Liquidity, Tax free dividends
High	Equity		

Their appeal is not just limited to these categories of investors. Specific goals like career planning for children and retirement plans are also catered to by mutual funds. Children funds have found their way in a big way with many of the fund houses already having launched a children fund. Essentially debt oriented, these schemes invite investments, which are locked till the child attains majority and requires money for higher education. You can invest today and assure financial support to your child when he/she requires them. The schemes have given very good returns of around 14 percent in the last one-year period. These schemes are also designed to provide tax efficiency. The returns generated by these funds come under capital gains and attract tax at concessional rates.

Besides this, if the objective was to save taxes, the industry offers equity linked savings schemes as well. Equity-based funds, they can take long-term call on stocks and market conditions without having to worry about redemption pressure as the money is locked in for three years and provide good returns. Some of the ELSS have been exceptional performers in past and cater to equity investor with good performances. The industry offered tax benefits under various sections of the IT Act. For e.g. dividend income is free in the hands of the investor while capital gains are taxed after providing for cost inflation indexation. Hitherto, the benefits under section 54 EA/EB were available to take benefits of the tax provisions for capital gains but have now been removed.

The benefits listed so far have essentially been for the small retail investor but the industry can attract investments from institutional and big investors as well. Liquid funds offer liquidity as well as better returns than banks and so attract investors. Many funds provide anytime withdrawal enabling a big investor to take maximum benefits.

Like we said earlier, the appeal of mutual funds cuts across investor classes. In other developed countries, mutual funds attract much more investments as compared to the banking sector but in India the case is reverse. We lack awareness about the benefits that are offered by these schemes. It is time that investors irrespective of their risk capacities, made intelligent decisions to generate better returns and mutual funds are definitely one of the ways to go about it.

THE GROUND RULES OF MUTUAL FUND INVESTING

Moses gave to his followers 10 commandments that were to be followed till eternity. The world of investments too has several ground rules meant for investors who are novices in their own right and wish to enter the myriad world of investments. These come in handy for there is every possibility of losing what one has if due care is not taken.

1. **Assess yourself:** Self-assessment of one's needs; expectations and risk profile is of prime importance failing which; one will make more mistakes in putting money in right places than otherwise. One should identify the degree of risk bearing capacity one has and also clearly state the expectations from the investments. Irrational expectations will only bring pain.

2. **Try to understand where the money is going:** It is important to identify the nature of investment

and to know if one is compatible with the investment. One can lose substantially if one picks the *wrong* kind of mutual fund. In order to avoid any confusion it is better to go through the literature such as offer document and fact sheets that mutual fund companies provide on their funds.

3. **Don't rush in picking funds, think first:** one first has to decide what he wants the money for and it is this investment goal that should be the guiding light for all investments done. It is thus important to know the risks associated with the fund and align it with the quantum of risk one is willing to take. One should take a look at the portfolio of the funds for the purpose. Excessive exposure to any specific sector should be avoided, as it will only add to the risk of the entire portfolio. Mutual funds invest with a certain ideology such as the "Value Principle" or "Growth Philosophy". Both have their share of critics but both philosophies

work for investors of different kinds. Identifying the proposed investment philosophy of the fund will give an insight into the kind of risks that it shall be taking in future.

4. **Invest. Don't speculate:** A common investor is limited in the degree of risk that he is willing to take. It is thus of key importance that there is thought given to the process of investment and to the time horizon of the intended investment. One should abstain from speculating which in other words would mean getting out of one fund and investing in another with the intention of making quick money. One would do well to remember that nobody can perfectly time the market so staying invested is the best option unless there are compelling reasons to exit.

5. **Don't put all the eggs in one basket:** This old age adage is of utmost importance. No matter what the risk profile of a person is, it is always advisable to diversify

the risks associated. So putting one's money in different asset classes is generally the best option as it averages the risks in each category. Thus, even investors of equity should be judicious and invest some portion of the investment in debt. Diversification even in any particular asset class (such as equity, debt) is good. Not all fund managers have the same acumen of fund management and with identification of the best man being a tough task, it is good to place money in the hands of several fund managers. This might reduce the maximum return possible, but will also reduce the risks.

6. **Be regular:** Investing should be a habit and not an exercise undertaken at one's wishes, if one has to really benefit from them. As we said earlier, since it is extremely difficult to know when to enter or exit the market, it is important to beat the market by being systematic. The basic philosophy of Rupee cost averaging

would suggest that if one invests regularly through the ups and downs of the market, he would stand a better chance of generating more returns than the market for the entire duration. The SIPs (Systematic Investment Plans) offered by all funds helps in being systematic. All that one needs to do is to give post-dated cheques to the fund and thereafter one will not be harried later. The Automatic investment Plans offered by some funds goes a step further, as the amount can be directly/electronically transferred from the account of the investor.

7. **Do your homework:**

It is important for all investors to research the avenues available to them irrespective of the investor category they belong to. This is important because an informed investor is in a better decision to make right decisions. Having identified the risks associated with the investment is important and so one should try to know all aspects associated with it. Asking the intermediaries is one of the ways to take care of the problem.

8. **Find the right funds**

Finding funds that do not charge much fees is of importance, as the fee charged ultimately goes from the pocket of the investor. This is even more important for debt funds as the returns from these funds are not much. Funds that charge more will reduce the yield to the investor. Finding the right funds is important and one should also use these funds for tax efficiency. Investors of equity should keep in mind that all dividends are currently tax-free in India and so their tax liabilities can be reduced if the dividend payout option is used. Investors of debt will be charged a tax on dividend distribution and so can easily avoid the payout options.

9. **Keep track of your investments**

Finding the right fund is important but even more important is to keep track of the way they are performing in the market. If the market is beginning to enter a bearish phase, then investors of equity too will benefit by switching to debt funds as the losses can be minimized. One can always switch back to equity if the equity market starts to show some buoyancy.

10. **Know when to sell your mutual funds:** Knowing when to exit a fund too is of utmost importance. One should book profits immediately when enough has been earned i.e. the initial expectation from the fund has been met with. Other factors like non-performance, hike in fee charged and change in any basic attribute of the fund etc. are some of the reasons for to

exit.Investments in mutual funds too are not risk-free and so investments warrant some caution and careful attention of the investor. Investing in mutual funds can be a dicey business for people who do not remember to follow these rules diligently, as people are likely to commit mistakes by being ignorant or adventurous enough to take risks more than what they can absorb. This is the reason why people would do well to remember these rules before they set out to invest their hard-earned money.

RISK MANAGEMENT AND MUTUAL FUND

The basic objective of a mutual fund is to provide a diversified portfolio so as to reduce the risk in investments at a lower cost. The mutual fund industry worldwide is based on this premise. Investors who take up mutual fund route for investments believe that their risk is minimized at lower costs, and they get an optimum portfolio of securities that match their risk appetite. They are ignorant about the diverse techniques and hedging products that can be used for minimizing the market volatility and hence take the help of the fund managers. It is very daunting to note that the drop in the NAV of some of the schemes is higher than the erosion of value in some of the ICE stocks. The recent survey conducted by PricewaterhouseCoopers (PWC) on risk management by mutual funds has posted interesting as well as worrying results. According to the survey, as many as 50 percent of the respondent mutual funds are not managing risk properly. If this is not all, 50 percent of the respondents did not even have documented risk procedures or dedicated risk managers. The respondents included among others, some of the heavyweights of the Indian MF industry viz.

Templeton, Alliance, Prudential and IDBI Principal MF.

Worrisome news it is, for the investor who still believes MFs are a route to manage one's money in a better and safe manner. The recent wild movements in the NAVs of several equity funds have belied all expectation of a diversified portfolio from the fund managers when the basic tenet behind portfolio management is risk management. Mr. Shyam Bhat, Fund Manager-Tata asset Management Ltd. said 'Indian Mutual fund industry is not using statistical techniques of risk management but is using diversification effectively within the market limitations. As far as use of derivatives is concerned, they are not presently used because of the low volumes, low liquidity and absence of sufficient hedging products in the market '.

Aggression has been the key word followed by the AMCs when it comes to taking positions in stocks. With investment in volatile ICE sectors being the driver of growth last season, almost everybody had taken big exposures to them. Birla MF maintained its exposures in Infosys to almost 25 percent in all of its equity schemes throughout last year. The same is true of ING Savings Trust that has Rs. 60 crores invested in

Wipro and Infosys out of the total fund size of 135 crores in its growth fund. The result of these exposures is that the fund witnessed a movement of almost 9 percent in a single day on budget when the market saw an appreciation of around 4.36 percent. In their quest for growth, many funds have seen very volatile movements in NAVs. The investor confidence may not be lost but such volatility sure dents it. The point is not whether AMCs should be chastised or not but just to question the practices as the fate of many investors is linked to it. An ordinary investor considers mutual funds as the experts in investment decisions and so naturally expects the decision of investing in mutual funds to bear fruit. However, AMCs often leave a lot to be desired as they falter on important fronts like NAV and portfolio disclosure besides posting high fluctuations and poor returns.

The Beta of some of the favorite stocks is shown below. The Table contains the Beta of some of the ICE scrips that constitute the top 10 holdings across various equity funds.

DSQ Software Ltd.	2.09	Taurus Libra Leap (5.68%), DSP ML Tech. (6.06%)
Satyam Computer Services Ltd.	2.00	ING Growth Port (11.2%), Alliance Equity Fund (9.7%), Chola freedom Tech (11.51%)
SSI Ltd.	1.98	IL&FS eCom (9.63%), LIC Dhansamridhi (9.18%)
Wipro Ltd.	1.87	ING Growth (23.8%), Magnum Sector Fund - Infotech (15%), Alliance Alliance New Millennium (10%)
Himachal Futuristic Communications Ltd.	1.82	UTI Sector-Services (9.48%), Taurus Discovery Stock (10.45%)
Global Tele-Systems Ltd.	1.81	UTI US 92 (7.02%), ING Growth Portfolio

		(3.8%)
Zee Telefilms Ltd.	1.70	UTI Sector-Services (7.21%), ING Growth Portfolio (10.06%),
Infosys Technologies Ltd.	1.54	ING Growth Portfolio (20.5%), Alliance New Millennium (11.5%)

As can be seen, some of the stocks are too volatile and can cause wild movements in the NAVs of funds that have taken exposures in them. The standard deviation of the returns in some of these funds points to it. While Alliance Equity Fund has a Standard Deviation of 2.53, Birla Advantage has its Standard Deviation at 2.57. ING Growth has a standard deviation of 3.3, which is relatively high due to its exposure to two volatile ICE scrips. Birla Advantage has reduced its exposures to Infosys drastically in the last two months and taken steps to contain volatility. Similar steps are being planned by SBI Mutual Fund that is recasting its equity portfolio to reduce risks as they can scare investors.

It is unfortunate that the fund managers are

not taking due care for minimizing the risk and are in a race to post higher and higher returns during the phase of bull-run. They should understand that the investors forget the high returns posted in any specific period very soon but they take hell lot of time to forget the burns they get during periods of losses. Hence for maintaining the confidence of the retail investors it is very important to control wild fluctuations in the NAVs. The basic technique of portfolio management thrusts on diversification, which preaches inclusion of negative beta, stocks in the portfolio so as to minimize the impact of fluctuation in the market. Diversification always has a cost and investors are willing to pay for it if it is properly done. The fund manager should disclose what they are doing at the hedging front. They should come up and tell their investors as to what they do at times of high fluctuations. Normally it has been seen that they outperform the broad market indices during the bull-runs and under-perform the indices during the bear-phases. The industry needs to revise their attitude and try to streamline their actions with their objectives. Some mutual fund houses are quite disciplined but every body should embrace the same spirit. There are some infrastructural problems but fund managers need to be more vigilant on the market movements. Mr. Bhupinder Sethi, Fund Manager - Dundee Mutual Fund said 'We are actively monitoring the market movements and taking calls accordingly. Though we are presently not using derivatives for hedging of risk because of lack of depth in the market for the product, but we go into cash when we see the expectations of huge corrections coming in.'

Poor performance, poor servicing to clients and failure of third party service providers, are the three major risk factors identified in the survey by PWC. These are also going to be crucial in a rapidly growing competitive scenario. Under this setting, it is not just growth that should be the focus area but also better management of all risks and hence, AMCs would do well to keep the investor and his interest in mind before taking any decision.

BOND FUND SOME BASICS

The recent upsurge in debt market has seen the performance of bond funds go up substantially. These funds hold major investments in bonds of different categories and so the downward change in yield has seen the returns from these funds soar high. However, despite the positive outcome, not many people know the mechanism and consequently are not aware of their pros and cons. We have just tried to explain what are bond funds and the factors that affect them.

What is a bond fund?
Debt funds by nature, bond funds like all mutual funds, are investment vehicles. They are meant especially for investors with relatively less appetite for risk and having an intention to earn returns higher than what are possible to earn from other avenues like Fixed Deposits that are considered as safe. So, safety and return both are of equal concern for those investing in Bond Funds. Most bond funds pay income regularly and their NAVs tend to fluctuate less than an equity fund.

Where do they invest?
In order to successfully achieve the goals of

the fund, they invest in a multiplicity of debt instruments such as Corporate pares, papers issued by GOI etc. with different maturities and qualities. In order to balance the liquidity needs of investors who might want to redeem their funds any time, they also have exposure to money market instruments and call papers. Generally, mutual funds invest in bonds issued by different issuers such as government, corporate houses etc. Bonds can be classified on the basis of their issuer as:

1. **Government Bonds**

   The Government Treasury and its agencies issue these bonds. Treasury bonds are considered the highest quality of all bonds because the credit of the government backs them and so the payment upon maturity is more or less guaranteed. In exchange for this very high margin of credit safety, they have the lowest yields.

2. **Corporate Bonds**

   These are issued by various companies to finance their operations, expansion activities etc. Credit rating agencies such as CRISIL, CARE, ICRA rate these instruments in India on the basis of their degree of safety, which is defined as their ability to pay the amount on maturity. The risk-return trade off is witnessed here as well, for companies with good rating offer less yield.

3. **Municipal bonds**

These bonds are issued by governments and municipalities. Considered as reasonably safe, these bonds provide varying returns depending upon their maturities.

What affects the yield of a Bond Fund?
The returns from a bond fund are essentially the weighted average of the returns on each of its investment. So if a fund has invested in bonds of different maturities and yields, the yield from the fund will be the weighted average of the yields on different securities, weighted by the proportion of invested sum. The quality of papers and average duration of the portfolio are some of the factors that determine the returns one can earn from the fund. However, the prices and yields of bonds can fluctuate like other investments and so there is some risk inherent even in bond funds

and they are not absolutely risk-free as they are often made out to be.

What are the risks associated?
Bond funds invest in bonds and like any investment are affected by some risks. There are several risks associated with bonds and so they also affect the funds that invest in bonds. They are:

Interest-rate risk
Unlike stock market where an upward movement of market leads to upward movement in stock prices, it is a fall in the market yield that pushes up the prices of debt securities. This happens because there exists an inverse relationship between the yield and the price of a bond. So, if there is an upward movement of interest rates after one has invested in a bond fund, the prices of bonds will go down leading to a corresponding fall in the NAVs of the bond funds. Let us take an example:

Suppose a person buys a bond for Rs. 100 with a coupon rate of 10 percent. In other terms the person should get Rs. 110 at the end of the year. If the RBI announces a hike in the bank rate and the market yield for the duration of the bond increased, say to 11 percent, the prices of the bond will fall around to Rs. 90.91 in order to adjust to the market yield. This is termed as interest rate risk in financial jargon and is precisely what happened in 2000 when RBI had hiked the interest rates.

An investor stands to benefit in the opposite scenario, when the interest rates are cut as then the prices go up leading to better returns from the fund. If the interest rate in the above example falls to 9 percent, a person still gets Rs. 10 in interest but in order to align the amount received to the prevailing market yield, the price of the bond adjusts to Rs. 111.11. In this case, the investor is better of by selling it at Rs. 111.11 than holding it to its maturity, as then he will only get Rs. 110.

This risk is also dependent upon the maturity and duration of the bond and generally, the longer a fund's duration or average maturity, the higher its interest-rate risk, or the more sensitive the NAV of the fund will be to changes in interest rates. One can reduce the interest rate risk by choosing a bond fund with a shorter duration or average maturity.

Credit risk

Just like shares where the performance of the company has some bearing on the stock prices, credibility of the issuer is of importance in debt instruments. The risk of the issuer not being able to make payments on his liabilities (debt instrument) is termed as default risk or credit risk. This is of special concern to the investor if the fund is investing into junk bonds or lower quality bonds. Bond funds offer professional management and a range of quality ratings to help lower this risk and so investors stand to benefit by the expertise of fund to pick good papers only.

Delay Risk

Cash flows are estimated on the basis of the pattern of income distribution. For example, a bond can pay interest half yearly, on fixed dates and so if there is any delay in receiving payments from the issuer, there is bound to be a mismatch between the cash flows. This can be termed as the delay risk. Mutual funds too can miss out on the interest due on an investment and have to show it as accrued but not received. This also affects the time value of the money due. A continuation of this trend may lead to a re-rating of the paper and add to the non-performing assets of the fund.

Balancing Risk vs. Reward

As with any investment in any category, there is always a trade-off between the risks taken and returns generated. The greater the risk of a bond fund (dependent on the quality and duration of papers), the higher is the potential reward, or return. With a bond fund, the risk that prices may fluctuate and the value of your investment may increase or decrease is not eliminated and so one must choose funds based on his risk tolerance.

WHEN TO SAY GOOD BYE TO MUTUAL FUND

While there are many investment consultants, some by profession, some self-professed, who suggest on when to invest in a particular avenue, there is a certain paucity of people who talk of when to exit. People looking to invest get in many options and mutual funds happen to be one such preferred destination for people who want more returns than their fixed deposits would earn them. It's also a preferred option for the people who are circumspect about investing into stocks directly and believe that mutual funds can manage risks and funds better than they could.

The recent crash will have several lessons for the investor but will not drive them away from the mutual funds in the wake of falling returns because they still are among the best investment avenues available to them. The primary of the lessons learnt is, not to chase returns. One of the biggest flaws in the process of investing is to chase the performance of funds alone. While they do give an indication to how well a fund can perform, they remain just indicative, for all good reasons. Take for example, the case of several equity funds that were riding sky-high between October 99 and March 2000. Alliance Equity Fund posted absolute returns of 168 percent between October 1, 99 and March 7, 2000. Birla Advantage posted 125 gains and ING Growth Fund posted mind-boggling returns of 193 percent during the same period. The recommendation by the consultants still remained "buy". However, investors who chased the returns of these schemes have learnt the bitter and eternal truth that "what goes up must come down", the hard way. These funds have posted negative returns of 64 percent, 61 percent and 82 percent respectively since peaking on the same day, March 7, 2000. And so, while chasing hot funds might be a good idea in a market that has started to rise, it certainly is a sure recipe to doom in a peaking market. The only people to have gained from investing in these schemes were the ones who exited while it was still profitable.

The others did not know when to exit and so we are just trying to put forward some situations when the investor should consider withdrawing their investments from the funds.

Fund is not performing
This reason for selling, although valid in certain

conditions, is where most investors make a mistake. When calculating performance one shouldn't look at too short a period and make a mistake by comparing apples to oranges.

It is important to base the decision on **relative performance** and not absolute performance. When one fund is down 5% while other funds or the market in general are up 10%, it is very tempting to switch over to what is "hot." Chasing Performance is the best way to shoot oneself in the foot as we just discussed above.

When studying **relative performance**, one should look at his fund and compare it to its peers. However, comparisons should be drawn between parallels and so equity funds can not and should not be compared with debt funds. When choosing a benchmark, one must select funds in the same category. If one's fund was down 2% and the average equity fund was down 4%, then there is no good enough reason to sell it. One should compare the returns posted by his fund with that of the peers across various horizons such as 1-year, 3-year and above. A short-term view can often lead to committing hara-kiri, as it doesn't present the full picture. If it has underperformed the average of its peers in all cases, then it sure is one of the better reasons to exit from the fund.

A change in life stage
Investments are done with a certain objective in mind and life stages are often a determining factor of what a person needs. A young man can afford to take more risks than a person nearing his retirement can. In such cases, it pays to withdraw money from the equity investments made earlier and put them in safer, more conservative debt funds that offer stable returns without compromising on risk. So a change in life stages would be one such reason to consider switching into a fund that matches with one's needs. As one nears retirement, one might want to consider more conservative funds. If one gets married, one might need to compromise one's risk tolerance and desired returns with that of the spouse. This could trigger off the need to exit.

A major change in any basic attribute of the fund
When the fund changes any basic attribute as mentioned by it in its offer documents, the investors have a choice of getting out of it. Even SEBI has provided for an exit route being made available to the investors. Changes like a change in Asset Management Company or in investment

style of fund or change of structure say from closed-end to open-end etc. are good enough reasons for an investor to consider switching or exiting from it as they are certainly likely to affect the fund in a major way.

Fund doesn't comply with its objective
One of the important parameters in the selection of the fund is alignment of the risk profiles of the investor and fund. The objective of the fund says a lot about how the fund plans to invest. If the objective is not being complied with, it is one of the exit points worth considering. For example, the three funds discussed above, Alliance Equity, Birla Advantage and ING Growth all claim to be diversified equity funds yet they had huge exposures to select ICE sector scrips that not only added volatility than is expected out of diversified funds but also in a way, went against their stated objective.

The Fund's Expense Ratio Rises
A small rise in an expense ratio is not a big deal, however a significant rise can result in substantial reduction of yields and so it would be better to exit the fund. In the case of bond funds or money market funds, it is highly unlikely that the fund can increase its returns enough to

justify an increase in the fund's expenses.

The Fund Manager Has Changed
A simple change of fund managers, in itself, is not enough reason to sell a fund on a short-term basis. If it is a passively managed fund (index fund), then one has little to no reason to worry. However, if it is an actively managed fund, then has to keep the eyes open on the new manager. Observing the styles, stock picking and risks undertaken by the new manager is important for it discloses a lot about how the fund might fare in the future. If satisfied, one will have no reason to complain later but the process needs time and so an investor has to observe the fund manager for some time before one takes a decision.

Enough has been earned
However, nothing is as important as to rein the horses in time. The primary principle behind safety of investment is to take risks that can be tolerated. The principle also is specific on the expectations that the investor must have from any investment. Just as it is important to set realistic targets that one hopes to achieve from the investment, it is also important to exit when target as expected has been achieved irrespective of the fact that it might be generating better returns in a short-term.

Waiting longer might not prove beneficial, as one need not be lucky all the time. Equity investments are volatile and it doesn't take long for the moods in the markets to swing either way. So, it would only be wise to move out when the going is still good. Otherwise, the investors sanguine of generating even higher returns than what the fund generated in its peak days, would be cursing themselves for not exiting.

The above list is certainly not exhaustive and individuals will have other better reasons to quit as well. It's just that most don't know when to apply thought and so these would come in handy.

MUTUAL FUND : HOPE FLOATS

The new millennium brought with itself what had rarely been seen in the market. Burgeoning growth. Riding on the ICE boom, the market touched great heights. Also touching new heights were the returns generated by equity funds. But as the saying goes, what goes up has to come down and the higher one goes the steeper is the fall.

This is exactly what the equity funds have experienced over the last one year as they have been robbed of their valuables by the volatile markets. The fall out of the volatile market conditions is reflected in significant erosion of the total assets under management of the equity funds.

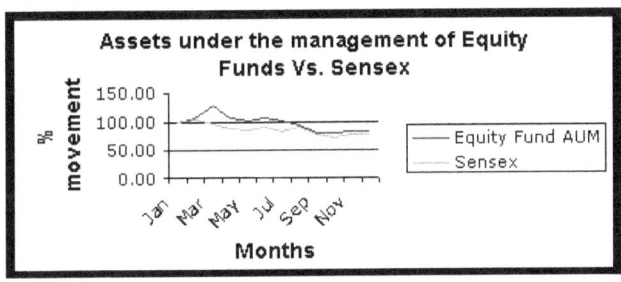

As can be seen, in the last one-year, equity funds have lost almost 18 percent of the wealth they had started the year with. Yet, surprisingly, they have managed to stay above the market that lost almost 26 percent in the same duration. So despite the fact that people have lost money in this year at a rate greater than the rate of depreciation of market capitalisation of the index, the funds have received some fresh inflows. The industry on the whole saw a cumulative inflow of Rs. 5962 crores through new issues and Rs. 81210 crores through existing schemes in the year but also saw redemption of Rs. 68514 crores in the same period.

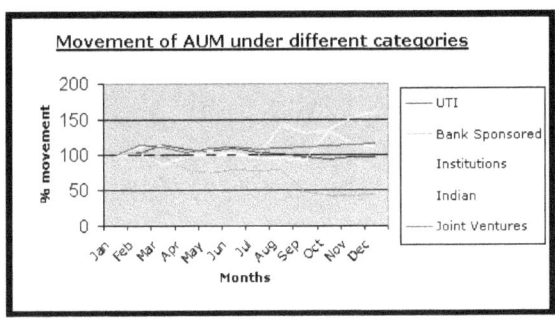

The same trends can be observed if we dissect the industry across different categories of fund houses. Assets under management of different categories of fund houses have moved diversely. The industry finished with lower assets under management as it lost almost 2 percent in the year while the industry giant UTI lost about 4.5 percent followed by Indian Joint Ventures at 4.1 percent. However, the category to have lost maximum in the year was that of Bank sponsored mutual funds that lost almost 56 percent. The poor performance in this category was not just due to the ICE bust as many would like to believe but also due to redemption of many schemes in the sector. However, the industry saw shifting patterns in the investor's preferences. The private sector mutual funds and foreign joint ventures struck big time this year and have emerged as the biggest gainers despite the market crash. Both the categories gained in excess of 30 percent and defied the general trend in the industry. This stresses the point that returns as well as quality of services matter to the investor. This had hitherto been not too significant till now but has become apparent now.

This is indeed reflective of maturing investors, though only just. Investors have been known to follow the herd mentality and sell off when the principal amount is under pressure. Although people have redeemed money from their investments in equity, by and large, more money has also flown in to the industry. With the markets looking to revive, the industry can still hope for better days, as investors seem to be gradually understanding that despite the correlation between the market and mutual funds, they are better placed with their risks reduced in mutual funds.

Source: Mutualfundsindia Research Team

Debt Funds: A golden horizon with annualised weekly return of 27.80%

The debt funds, which hold the major market share of mutual fund industry, have again started to smile at the investors with mind boggling returns they have posted in the last week. The market sentiments are also conducive for the promoters of debt funds. All of the macro indicators are favorable. The average annualised returns posted by the top 50 debt funds in the last seven days period was astounding 27.80% with the top position held by KP Pension Plan. The annualised return posted by the fund is astronomical and hence not quoted here, else would send ripples to the heart of investors who have kept themselves away from mutual fund industry after burning their fingers in the recent past when debt funds gave negative returns.

The returns posted by the top ten open ended debt funds as on Jan 9, 2001 are shown below.

ual Fund Name	Last 7 days' Return	
	Absolute	Annual
ension Plan	2.38	240.91
hildren Asset Gift Plan	1.43	109.67
Debt Fund	1.07	74.19
ıce MIP	0.7	43.87
pleton MIP	0.65	40.19
Bond Wholesale	0.62	38.03
Bond Deposit	0.59	35.90
iquid	0.59	35.90
ılays Super Saver Income	0.59	35.90
ıce Liquid Income -Dividend	0.58	35

As on Jan 9, 2001 It might be thought that this is a momentous issue and the returns would go down, but the macro economic indicators are all suggesting a phase of softening of interest rate on anvil. Call rates are hovering in the band of 9.75% - 10.25% for most part of the week. Players in the G'Sec market are building fresh positions. There has been a correction in the yield curve in short to medium term when the yield has dipped by nearly 16-20 basis points. On Jan 4, 2001 the bond prices shot up sharply following a sentiment driven rally after the US Fed reserve cut interest rate by 50 basis points. Gilt/ bond prices rallied by around 80 – 100 paisa as traders started buying heavily in the market on hopes of RBI cutting bank rates. The measures taken by the RBI on Friday of scrapping the interest rate surcharge of 50% on import finance and the 25% interest rate to be charged on overdue export bills further improved sentiments in the market. YTM of ten-year benchmark paper has dipped to 10.8% from10.96% at the start of the week. Forex reserve is at all-time high of around $40 billion. Considering the positive sentiment in the market coupled with easy call rates bidding interest is likely to continue in the gilt and bond market and would push the NAVs of the bond funds further. The sentiments got a boost on the indication of the RBI governor Mr. Bimal Jalan that the individual banks are free to revise the interest rates.

These macro economic indicators are suggesting a major re-rating of debt papers and will reflect in the returns of the debt mutual funds. Most of the fund managers have increased their portfolio duration drastically in anticipation of softening of interest rate and are getting results in the form of upward correction in their NAVs on mark to market operation. Mr. Sanjeev Bhasin at Dundee Mutual Fund is of the opinion that there is not much threat in the interest rate regime of the economy and the present scenario will persist atleast till the budget is announced and the central bank comes up with fresh borrowing programme. Though this type of return might be misleading for investors if they expect the same returns for the longer period of time, but it can be opined with confidence that the returns that these funds are going to post will be better than that in the previous quarter and the good phase will persist atleast during the present quarter of the financial year.

PERFORMANCE MEASURES OF MUTUAL FUND

Mutual Fund industry today, with about 34 players and more than five hundred schemes, is one of the most preferred investment avenues in India. However, with a plethora of schemes to choose from, the retail investor faces problems in selecting funds. Factors such as investment strategy and management style are qualitative, but the funds record is an important indicator too. Though past performance alone can not be indicative of future performance, it is, frankly, the only quantitative way to judge how good a fund is at present. Therefore, there is a need to correctly assess the past performance of different mutual funds.

Worldwide, good mutual fund companies over are known by their AMCs and this fame is directly linked to their superior stock selection skills. For mutual funds to grow, AMCs must be held accountable for their selection of stocks. In other words, there must be some performance indicator that will reveal the quality of stock selection of various AMCs.

Return alone should not be considered as the

basis of measurement of the performance of a mutual fund scheme, it should also include the risk taken by the fund manager because different funds will have different levels of risk attached to them. Risk associated with a fund, in a general, can be defined as variability or fluctuations in the returns generated by it. The higher the fluctuations in the returns of a fund during a given period, higher will be the risk associated with it. These fluctuations in the returns generated by a fund are resultant of two guiding forces. First, general market fluctuations, which affect all the securities present in the market, called market risk or systematic risk and second, fluctuations due to specific securities present in the portfolio of the fund, called unsystematic risk. The Total Risk of a given fund is sum of these two and is measured in terms of standard deviation of returns of the fund. Systematic risk, on the other hand, is measured in terms of Beta, which represents fluctuations in the NAV of the fund vis-à-vis market. The more responsive the NAV of a mutual fund is to the changes in the market; higher will be its beta. Beta is calculated by relating the returns on a mutual fund with the returns in the market. While unsystematic risk can be diversified through investments in a number of instruments, systematic risk can not. By using the risk return relationship, we try to assess the competitive strength of the mutual funds vis-à-vis one another in a better way.

In order to determine the risk-adjusted returns of investment portfolios, several eminent authors have worked since 1960s to develop composite performance indices to evaluate a portfolio by comparing alternative portfolios within a particular risk class. The most important and widely used measures of performance are:

Ø The Treynor Measure
Ø The Sharpe Measure
Ø Jenson Model
Ø Fama Model

The Treynor Measure
Developed by Jack Treynor, this performance measure evaluates funds on the basis of Treynor's Index. This Index is a ratio of return generated by the fund over and above risk free rate of return (generally taken to be the return on securities backed by the government, as there is no credit risk associated), during a given period and systematic risk associated with it (beta). Symbolically, it can be represented as:

Treynor's Index (Ti) = (Ri - Rf)/Bi.

Where, Ri represents return on fund, Rf is risk free rate of return and Bi is beta of the fund.

All risk-averse investors would like to maximize

this value. While a high and positive Treynor's Index shows a superior risk-adjusted performance of a fund, a low and negative Treynor's Index is an indication of unfavorable performance.

The Sharpe Measure

In this model, performance of a fund is evaluated on the basis of Sharpe Ratio, which is a ratio of returns generated by the fund over and above risk free rate of return and the total risk associated with it. According to Sharpe, it is the total risk of the fund that the investors are concerned about. So, the model evaluates funds on the basis of reward per unit of total risk. Symbolically, it can be written as:

Sharpe Index $(Si) = (Ri - Rf)/Si$

Where, Si is standard deviation of the fund.

While a high and positive Sharpe Ratio shows a superior risk-adjusted performance of a fund, a low and negative Sharpe Ratio is an indication of unfavorable performance.

Comparison of Sharpe and Treynor

Sharpe and Treynor measures are similar in a way, since they both divide the risk premium by a numerical risk measure. The total risk is appropriate when we are evaluating the risk return relationship for well-diversified portfolios. On the other hand, the systematic risk is the relevant measure of risk when we are evaluating less than fully diversified portfolios or individual stocks. For a well-diversified portfolio the total risk is equal to systematic risk. Rankings based on total risk (Sharpe measure) and systematic risk (Treynor measure) should be identical for a well-diversified portfolio, as the total risk is reduced to systematic risk. Therefore, a poorly diversified fund that ranks higher on Treynor measure, compared with another fund that is highly diversified, will rank lower on Sharpe Measure.

Jenson Model

Jenson's model proposes another risk adjusted performance measure. This measure was developed by Michael Jenson and is sometimes referred to as the Differential Return Method. This measure involves evaluation of the returns that the fund has generated vs. the returns actually expected out of the fund given the level of its systematic risk. The surplus between the two returns is called Alpha, which measures the performance of a fund compared with the actual returns over the period. Required return of a fund at a given level of risk (Bi) can be calculated as:

$Ri = Rf + Bi (Rm - Rf)$

Where, Rm is average market return during the given period. After calculating it, alpha can be obtained by subtracting required return from the actual return of the fund.

Higher alpha represents superior performance of the fund and vice versa. Limitation of this model is that it considers only systematic risk not the entire risk associated with the fund and an ordinary investor can not mitigate unsystematic risk, as his knowledge of market is primitive.

Fama Model

The Eugene Fama model is an extension of Jenson model. This model compares the performance, measured in terms of returns, of a fund with the required return commensurate with the total risk associated with it. The difference between these two is taken as a measure of the performance of the fund and is called net selectivity.

The net selectivity represents the stock selection skill of the fund manager, as it is the excess return over and above the return required to compensate for the total risk taken by the fund manager. Higher value of which indicates that fund manager has earned returns well above the return commensurate with the level of risk taken by him.

Required return can be calculated as: $Ri = Rf + Si/Sm*(Rm - Rf)$

Where, Sm is standard deviation of market returns. The net selectivity is then calculated by subtracting this required return from the actual return of the fund.

Among the above performance measures, two models namely, Treynor measure and Jenson model use systematic risk based on the premise that the unsystematic risk is diversifiable. These models are suitable for large investors like institutional investors with high risk taking capacities as they do not face paucity of funds and can invest in a number of options to dilute some risks. For them, a portfolio can be spread across a number of stocks and sectors. However, Sharpe measure and Fama model that consider the entire risk associated with fund are suitable for small investors, as the ordinary investor lacks the necessary skill and resources to diversified. Moreover, the selection of the fund on the basis of superior stock selection ability of the fund manager will also help in safeguarding the money invested to a great extent. The investment in funds that have generated big returns at higher levels of risks leaves the money all the more prone to risks of all kinds that may exceed the individual investors' risk appetite.

www.ingramcontent.com/pod-product-compliance
Lightning Source LLC
Chambersburg PA
CBHW070920180526
45168CB00005B/2081